'your wilderness awaits, get up early and get on your way'

My best sketch of
the view...

Doodles of the day...

Date:

Start Details:

Finish Details:

Who was walking
with me?

How were the
views?

Where we ate and
drank!

Thoughts along the
way!

My best sketch of
the view...

Doodles of the day...

Date:

Start Details:

Finish Details:

Who was walking
with me?

How were the
views?

Where we ate and
drank!

Thoughts along the
way!

My best sketch of
the view...

Doodles of the day...

Date:

Start Details:

Finish Details:

Who was walking
with me?

How were the
views?

Where we ate and
drank!

Thoughts along the
way!

My best sketch of
the view...

Doodles of the day...

Date:

Start Details:

Finish Details:

Who was walking
with me?

How were the
views?

Where we ate and
drank!

Thoughts along the
way!

My best sketch of
the view...

Doodles of the day...

Date:

Start Details:

Finish Details:

Who was walking
with me?

How were the
views?

Where we ate and
drank!

Thoughts along the
way!

My best sketch of
the view…

Doodles of the day…

Date:

Start Details:

Finish Details:

Who was walking
with me?

How were the
views?

Where we ate and
drank!

Thoughts along the
way!

My best sketch of
the view...

Doodles of the day...

Date:

Start Details:

Finish Details:

Who was walking
with me?

How were the
views?

Where we ate and
drank!

Thoughts along the
way!

My best sketch of
the view...

Doodles of the day...

Date:

Start Details:

Finish Details:

Who was walking
with me?

How were the
views?

Where we ate and
drank!

Thoughts along the
way!

My best sketch of
the view...

Doodles of the day...

Date:

Start Details:

Finish Details:

Who was walking
with me?

How were the
views?

Where we ate and
drank!

Thoughts along the
way!

My best sketch of
the view...

Doodles of the day...

Date:

Start Details:

Finish Details:

Who was walking
with me?

How were the
views?

Where we ate and
drank!

Thoughts along the
way!

My best sketch of
the view...

Doodles of the day...

Date:

Start Details:

Finish Details:

Who was walking
with me?

How were the
views?

Where we ate and
drank!

Thoughts along the
way!

My best sketch of
the view...

Doodles of the day...

Date:

Start Details:

Finish Details:

Who was walking
with me?

How were the
views?

Where we ate and
drank!

Thoughts along the
way!

My best sketch of
the view...

Doodles of the day...

Date:

Start Details:

Finish Details:

Who was walking
with me?

How were the
views?

Where we ate and
drank!

Thoughts along the
way!

My best sketch of
the view...

Doodles of the day...

Date:

Start Details:

Finish Details:

Who was walking
with me?

How were the
views?

Where we ate and
drank!

Thoughts along the
way!

My best sketch of
the view...

Doodles of the day...

Date:

Start Details:

Finish Details:

Who was walking
with me?

How were the
views?

Where we ate and
drank!

Thoughts along the
way!

My best sketch of
the view...

Doodles of the day...

Date:

Start Details:

Finish Details:

Who was walking
with me?

How were the
views?

Where we ate and
drank!

Thoughts along the
way!

My best sketch of
the view...

Doodles of the day...

Date:

Start Details:

Finish Details:

Who was walking
with me?

How were the
views?

Where we ate and
drank!

Thoughts along the
way!

My best sketch of
the view...

Doodles of the day...

Date:

Start Details:

Finish Details:

Who was walking
with me?

How were the
views?

Where we ate and
drank!

Thoughts along the
way!

My best sketch of
the view...

Doodles of the day...

Date:

Start Details:

Finish Details:

Who was walking
with me?

How were the
views?

Where we ate and
drank!

Thoughts along the
way!

My best sketch of
the view...

Doodles of the day...

Date:

Start Details:

Finish Details:

Who was walking
with me?

How were the
views?

Where we ate and
drank!

Thoughts along the
way!

My best sketch of
the view...

Doodles of the day...

Date:

Start Details:

Finish Details:

Who was walking
with me?

How were the
views?

Where we ate and
drank!

Thoughts along the
way!

My best sketch of
the view...

Doodles of the day...

Date:

Start Details:

Finish Details:

Who was walking
with me?

How were the
views?

Where we ate and
drank!

Thoughts along the
way!

My best sketch of
the view...

Doodles of the day...

Date:

Start Details:

Finish Details:

Who was walking
with me?

How were the
views?

Where we ate and
drank!

Thoughts along the
way!

My best sketch of
the view...

Doodles of the day...

Date:

Start Details:

Finish Details:

Who was walking
with me?

How were the
views?

Where we ate and
drank!

Thoughts along the
way!

My best sketch of
the view...

Doodles of the day...

Date:

Start Details:

Finish Details:

Who was walking
with me?

How were the
views?

Where we ate and
drank!

Thoughts along the
way!

My best sketch of
the view...

Doodles of the day...

Date:

Start Details:

Finish Details:

Who was walking
with me?

How were the
views?

Where we ate and
drank!

Thoughts along the
way!

My best sketch of
the view...

Doodles of the day...

Date:

Start Details:

Finish Details:

Who was walking
with me?

How were the
views?

Where we ate and
drank!

Thoughts along the
way!

My best sketch of
the view...

Doodles of the day...

Date:

Start Details:

Finish Details:

Who was walking
with me?

How were the
views?

Where we ate and
drank!

Thoughts along the
way!

My best sketch of
the view...

Doodles of the day...

Date:

Start Details:

Finish Details:

Who was walking
with me?

How were the
views?

Where we ate and
drank!

Thoughts along the
way!

My best sketch of
the view...

Doodles of the day...

Date:

Start Details:

Finish Details:

Who was walking
with me?

How were the
views?

Where we ate and
drank!

Thoughts along the
way!

My best sketch of
the view...

Doodles of the day...

Date:

Start Details:

Finish Details:

Who was walking
with me?

How were the
views?

Where we ate and
drank!

Thoughts along the
way!

My best sketch of
the view...

Doodles of the day...

Date:

Start Details:

Finish Details:

Who was walking
with me?

How were the
views?

Where we ate and
drank!

Thoughts along the
way!

My best sketch of
the view...

Doodles of the day...

Date:

Start Details:

Finish Details:

Who was walking
with me?

How were the
views?

Where we ate and
drank!

Thoughts along the
way!

My best sketch of
the view...

Doodles of the day...

Date:

Start Details:

Finish Details:

Who was walking
with me?

How were the
views?

Where we ate and
drank!

Thoughts along the
way!

My best sketch of
the view...

Doodles of the day...

Date:

Start Details:

Finish Details:

Who was walking
with me?

How were the
views?

Where we ate and
drank!

Thoughts along the
way!

My best sketch of
the view...

Doodles of the day...

Date:

Start Details:

Finish Details:

Who was walking
with me?

How were the
views?

Where we ate and
drank!

Thoughts along the
way!

My best sketch of
the view...

Doodles of the day...

Date:

Start Details:

Finish Details:

Who was walking
with me?

How were the
views?

Where we ate and
drank!

Thoughts along the
way!

My best sketch of
the view...

Doodles of the day...

Date:

Start Details:

Finish Details:

Who was walking
with me?

How were the
views?

Where we ate and
drank!

Thoughts along the
way!

My best sketch of
the view...

Doodles of the day...

Date:

Start Details:

Finish Details:

Who was walking
with me?

How were the
views?

Where we ate and
drank!

Thoughts along the
way!

My best sketch of
the view...

Doodles of the day...

Date:

Start Details:

Finish Details:

Who was walking
with me?

How were the
views?

Where we ate and
drank!

Thoughts along the
way!

My best sketch of
the view...

Doodles of the day...

Date:

Start Details:

Finish Details:

Who was walking
with me?

How were the
views?

Where we ate and
drank!

Thoughts along the
way!

My best sketch of
the view...

Doodles of the day...

Date:

Start Details:

Finish Details:

Who was walking
with me?

How were the
views?

Where we ate and
drank!

Thoughts along the
way!

My best sketch of
the view...

Doodles of the day...

Date:

Start Details:

Finish Details:

Who was walking
with me?

How were the
views?

Where we ate and
drank!

Thoughts along the
way!

My best sketch of
the view...

Doodles of the day...

Date:

Start Details:

Finish Details:

Who was walking
with me?

How were the
views?

Where we ate and
drank!

Thoughts along the
way!

My best sketch of
the view...

Doodles of the day...

Date:

Start Details:

Finish Details:

Who was walking
with me?

How were the
views?

Where we ate and
drank!

Thoughts along the
way!

My best sketch of
the view...

Doodles of the day...

Date:

Start Details:

Finish Details:

Who was walking
with me?

How were the
views?

Where we ate and
drank!

Thoughts along the
way!

My best sketch of
the view...

Doodles of the day...

Date:

Start Details:

Finish Details:

Who was walking
with me?

How were the
views?

Where we ate and
drank!

Thoughts along the
way!

My best sketch of
the view...

Doodles of the day...

Date:

Start Details:

Finish Details:

Who was walking
with me?

How were the
views?

Where we ate and
drank!

Thoughts along the
way!

My best sketch of
the view...

Doodles of the day...

Date:

Start Details:

Finish Details:

Who was walking
with me?

How were the
views?

Where we ate and
drank!

Thoughts along the
way!

My best sketch of
the view...

Doodles of the day...

Date:

Start Details:

Finish Details:

Who was walking
with me?

How were the
views?

Where we ate and
drank!

Thoughts along the
way!

My best sketch of
the view…

Doodles of the day…

Date:

Start Details:

Finish Details:

Who was walking
with me?

How were the
views?

Where we ate and
drank!

Thoughts along the
way!

My best sketch of
the view...

Doodles of the day...

Date:

Start Details:

Finish Details:

Who was walking
with me?

How were the
views?

Where we ate and
drank!

Thoughts along the
way!

Printed in Great Britain
by Amazon